Tons of Cakes.

by Jenny Alexander

THE CAST

DONUT and **CLEO**

brother and sister

COLIN

Donut and Cleo's stepdad

MUM

a very bad cook

UNCLE KEN

ICARUS

a parrot

Scene 1

The living room. Duncan, Cleo and Mum are sitting around. Icarus is on his perch.

CLEO   I'm bored.

DONUT   So am I.

CLEO   We've been waiting for ages.

MUM   They've probably got stuck in the traffic. Why don't you two go to the park for half an hour?

DONUT   We want to be here when they arrive.

MUM   Colin's uncle won't mind if you aren't here. He's staying for a couple of weeks, so there will be plenty of time for you to get to know him.

DONUT   What's he like, Colin's uncle?

MUM   I don't know. I've never met him. But Colin's very fond of him, so he must be all right.

CLEO   I'm going to be a cat when he gets here. I'm going to sit on his knee!

MUM	No, Cleo. You can't start jumping all over the poor man as soon as he arrives. He hasn't been well. That's why he's coming to stay with us, so that we can look after him.
DONUT	But Colin said it's ages since Uncle Ken broke his legs. He's got the plasters off and everything. He should be better by now.
CLEO	When Sasha in my class broke her leg it got better in no time.
MUM	Yes, but Sasha's only seven. When you're older, like Uncle Ken, it takes much longer to get over things. You need plenty of TLC, to help you get back on your feet again.

CLEO	What's TLC?
MUM	Tender Loving Care.
DONUT	Oh, yuk!
MUM	Never mind, Duncan. We're also going to give him a different sort of TLC you might like better – Tons of Lovely Cakes!

Doorbell rings. Donut and Cleo make faces at each other behind Mum's back, as she gets up to open the door. Uncle Ken hobbles in on two walking sticks, with Colin helping him.

COLIN	Here he is, everyone ... meet Uncle Ken!
MUM	I'm Cassandra. It's lovely to meet you, Ken. Colin has told us so much about you.

DONUT	I'm Donut, and this is Cleo.
CLEO	No it isn't. I'm not Cleo. I'm a cat. Miaow!
UNCLE KEN	I like cats. What's your name, puss?
CLEO	Marion.
DONUT	Whoever heard of a cat called Marion?
UNCLE KEN	I think it's a fine name. Hello, Marion.
CLEO	Miaow!
ICARUS	This is the nine o'clock news.
UNCLE KEN	Who said that?
DONUT	Icarus. He's our parrot. Do you like parrots, Uncle Ken?
UNCLE KEN	I don't know. I don't think I've ever met one. He must be very clever, to be able to talk.
DONUT	Not really. He never says anything interesting. He just copies things he hears.
COLIN	But that **is** clever for a parrot, Donut. Most parrots just say 'Pretty Polly'.
ICARUS	Pretty Polly!

MUM	Don't get excited, Icarus, or I'll put the blanket over you.
CLEO	The blanket makes him think it's night-time. Then he goes to sleep.
DONUT	I thought you were supposed to be a cat. Cats can't talk.
CLEO	**Pretend** cats can. Silly!
COLIN	Don't start arguing you two. What will Uncle Ken think, the minute he arrives!
MUM	Would you like a cup of tea, Ken? I've made a special cake for you.
UNCLE KEN	Ooh, lovely! Thank you very much.
ICARUS	Ooh, lovely! Thank you very much!

Scene 2

Same scene. Donut and Cleo on their own with Uncle Ken.
Icarus on his perch.

UNCLE KEN	It's nice of your mother to bake a cake for me.
DONUT	Ye-e-es ...
UNCLE KEN	What sort is it?
DONUT	I'm not sure.
CLEO	We're never sure.
UNCLE KEN	Well, it doesn't matter, because I love all sorts of cakes. *Colin comes in carrying a tea tray.*
COLIN	Here we are. A nice cup of tea.
UNCLE KEN	Ah! There's nothing like a cup of tea! *Mum comes in carrying a very odd-looking cake.*
MUM	And here's the cake.
DONUT	Ah! There's nothing like Mum's cakes!
UNCLE KEN	It looks ... interesting.
COLIN	Cassandra's cakes always look interesting.

MUM	I expect you'd like a big slice, Ken. You must be hungry after all that travelling.
UNCLE KEN	Well ...
MUM	Don't worry. There's still plenty left for us. *She hands him a plate with a huge slice of cake. He takes a bite.*
UNCLE KEN	It tastes ...
MUM	Unusual? I know. I make up all my own recipes. It's much more exciting.
UNCLE KEN	Do you do a lot of cooking, Cassandra?

MUM	Not as much as I'd like to. I don't usually have the time. But I've decided to stay at home and look after you, so I'll be able to bake every day while you're here.
UNCLE KEN	Oh ... good!
CLEO	Tell us how you hurt your legs, Uncle Ken.
UNCLE KEN	Well, I broke the first one falling over my cat. She was having a snooze on the stairs.
CLEO	**I'm** not the kind of cat that snoozes on the stairs.
UNCLE KEN	I'm delighted to hear that, Marion.
DONUT	Cleo's the kind of cat that just gets on your nerves.
COLIN	Duncan!
MUM	How did you break the other one, Ken?
UNCLE KEN	It was the day I got the plaster off. I tripped over outside the hospital. I didn't want to break my bad leg again, so I tried to fall on the other side ...
MUM	And broke that one! You poor thing! Have some more cake.
COLIN	He hasn't finished that piece yet.

UNCLE KEN   I'm afraid I may not manage it all. Would either of you children like to help me out?

DONUT   No thank you, Uncle Ken.

CLEO   You'll have to eat it all yourself.
Uncle picks up the cake, but pauses before putting it in his mouth.

UNCLE KEN   I say! Is that a cuckoo in the middle of your lawn?
They rush to the window. He gives the cake to Icarus, who eats it.

MUM   No, it's just a crisp packet. More tea, Uncle Ken?

UNCLE KEN   Ooh, lovely. Thank you very much!

ICARUS   (*Eating the cake*) Ooh, lovely. Thank you very much!

Scene 3

A week later. Cleo and Donut are standing beside Icarus's cage. Cleo has just taken the blanket off, and opened the door.

CLEO	Come on, Icarus.
DONUT	Doesn't he want to come out?
CLEO	No. He's just sitting there looking sorry for himself.
DONUT	He's sitting there looking fat, you mean!
CLEO	We've got to stop Uncle Ken giving him so much cake.
DONUT	He's been doing it for a whole week now.
CLEO	I can't believe Mum and Colin are still falling for that old cuckoo-on-the-lawn trick.
ICARUS	Is that a cuckoo in the middle of your lawn?
DONUT	Poor parrot. You're too silly to know what's good for you.
CLEO	And Mum's planning to make cupcakes today ...
DONUT	Oh, no! Not her famous cupcakes! They look like cakes but they taste like cups!

CLEO   Only harder!
Uncle Ken shuffles in, leaning on his sticks.

UNCLE KEN   What's up, kids?

DONUT   We're worried about Icarus. He won't come out of his cage.

CLEO   We think he might be ill. You shouldn't keep feeding him cake, you know.

UNCLE KEN   Ah! You noticed, then.

CLEO   He's not allowed to have cakes.

DONUT   It's one of the perks of being a parrot.

UNCLE KEN	But your mother's cakes are ... well ...
DONUT	Awful. We know.
CLEO	You'll just have to ask her to stop making them for you. Tell her you aren't very fond of cakes.
UNCLE KEN	I've tried. But she just thinks I'm worried about putting her to too much trouble. She says, "Honestly, Ken. It's no trouble at all!"
DONUT	So what are we going to do?
CLEO	Icarus is getting fatter and fatter.
UNCLE KEN	And I'm getting thinner and thinner. Your mum's a wonderful person, but her home cooking is killing me!
ICARUS	Killing me. Ohhh ... *Mum comes in.*
MUM	I've just been chatting to Trish Macdonald, and guess what? She says it's the wrong time of year for cuckoos.
UNCLE KEN	That's odd.
MUM	She reckons it might be a chicken you keep seeing, Ken.
DONUT	A chicken?

MUM	Yes. It seems the people at Number 35 have lost one.
DONUT	Are you saying Uncle Ken can't tell the difference between a cuckoo and a chicken?
MUM	It's an easy enough mistake to make.
DONUT	If you've got your eyes shut!
ICARUS	Aargh ... *Icarus falls off his perch. They all crowd round.*
MUM	Oh, my goodness! What's wrong with Icarus?
CLEO	He's dead!
DONUT	No he isn't. Don't make such a fuss.
MUM	Colin! Colin! Come quick! Icarus isn't well! *Colin rushes in.*
COLIN	What's wrong with him?
MUM	I don't know! But look at him!
COLIN	We've got to get him to the vet.
MUM	Pass me his blanket.
CLEO	He's dead! He's dead! *She burst into tears.*

MUM	Getting into a state is not going to help. You've got to be a big girl, Cleo. You and Donut will have to look after Uncle Ken while we take Icarus to the vet.
COLIN	Wipe your eyes, Princess. Everything's going to be fine. *He hands her a tissue. Mum is wrapping Icarus in his blanket.*

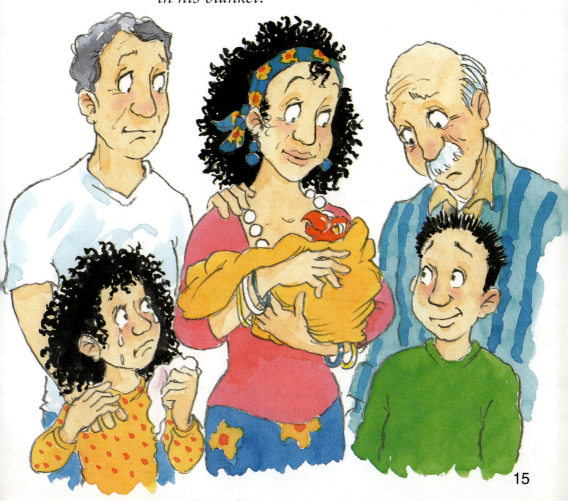

Scene 4

Cleo, Donut and Uncle Ken.

CLEO   Poor Icarus.

DONUT   He's got cake poisoning.

UNCLE KEN   This is more serious than I thought.

DONUT   One thing's for sure – you definitely can't go
on giving him cake.

UNCLE KEN   Well, then. There's only one thing for it. Your
mum keeps making cakes to build me up
and get me back on my feet again ...

DONUT   So?

UNCLE KEN   So if we want her to stop, I'm just going to
have to get back on my feet right now.

CLEO   How are you going to do that?

UNCLE KEN   Where there's a will there's a way. Take my
walking sticks and hide them, Cleo.

CLEO   Are you sure?

UNCLE KEN   Yes. My doctor says I should be able to
manage without them. I've just been too
scared of falling over again to try.
Cleo takes the walking sticks and runs out.

UNCLE KEN   Now clear the floor, Donut. We've got some walking to do!
They start walking about the room.

UNCLE KEN   Ooh, ouch! Ooh, ouch! Ooh, ouch!

DONUT   Are you sure you're all right, Uncle Ken?

UNCLE KEN   It's a bit painful.
Cleo comes back from hiding the walking sticks.

DONUT   Try thinking about something else while you walk. It'll take your mind off the pain.

CLEO	I know! You can pretend to be the Grand Old Duke of York, and we'll be the ten thousand men! *They all march round the room singing "The Grand Old Duke of York". Uncle Ken stops suddenly and points out the window.*
UNCLE KEN	Is that a chicken in the middle of your lawn?
DONUT	We're not falling for that one!
CLEO	You just want us to go out and look for it …
DONUT	… So that you can stop marching and have a rest.
UNCLE KEN	No, really. Look! *They go to the window.*
CLEO	It **is** a chicken!
DONUT	Let's go and catch it! *The children dash out.*
UNCLE KEN	Wait for me! *He follows them.*

Scene 5

The back garden. Colin is searching for the children and Uncle Ken. Icarus is watching through the open living room window.

COLIN   Where can they have got to? Cleo! Donut! Uncle Ken!
Mum comes racing out, carrying Uncle Ken's walking sticks.

MUM   I've found Ken's walking sticks.

COLIN   Where were they?

MUM   In the airing cupboard.

COLIN   In the airing cupboard?

MUM   Yes.

COLIN   What on earth is going on?
Donut, Cleo and Uncle Ken come through the garden gate. Mum runs over.

MUM   Where have you been? We've been so worried.

CLEO   We were taking the chicken back.

DONUT   Yes. You were right – it **was** a chicken that Uncle Ken kept seeing.

CLEO	And he saw it again.
DONUT	So we went out and caught it.
CLEO	Uncle Ken was great. He knew exactly how to pick it up.
DONUT	You have to make sure its wings are folded flat against its body.
CLEO	Otherwise it flaps and you can't hold onto it.
MUM	But what was Uncle Ken doing chasing a chicken around the garden?
COLIN	He could hardly walk this morning!

MUM	And what were his walking sticks doing in the airing cupboard?
CLEO	I put them there. I hid them.
MUM	That was very naughty, Cleo.
UNCLE KEN	No, no. I asked her to hide them.
COLIN	You asked her to hide them?
DONUT	Uncle Ken decided it was time he got back on his feet again.
CLEO	It really hurt at first ...
DONUT	... But then we saw the chicken ...
UNCLE KEN	... And they couldn't get hold of her ...
CLEO	So Uncle Ken had to come and help.
UNCLE KEN	That chicken was pretty quick on her feet!
ICARUS	This parrot is too fat! *They all turn and notice Icarus in the window.*
CLEO	Icarus! You're back!
DONUT	He looks a lot better.
CLEO	What did the vet say, Mum?
MUM	The vet said, "This parrot is too fat."

COLIN	It seems that Icarus has been eating too much.
MUM	Which is odd, because we always give him the same amount of parrot seed, and he's never had any problems before.
COLIN	Anyway, he's got to go on a diet.
DONUT	Poor Icarus!
ICARUS	Poor Icarus!
MUM	Talking about diets, I'd better go in and make some tea. You must all be starving.
UNCLE KEN	No, we're fine thank you, Cassandra. The lady at Number 35 was so pleased to have her chicken back, she made a huge plateful of scones for us.
MUM	Well, that's good. I do feel a bit tired.
DONUT	I'll get you a chair. *He gets a garden chair from the shed. Cleo gets one for Uncle Ken.*
UNCLE KEN	You've been very kind to me, Cassandra. You've made me feel really welcome, and I'm very grateful.
MUM	It's no trouble at all, Ken. You know that.

UNCLE KEN	Yes, but now I'm feeling better, I don't want you spending all your time looking after me any more.
MUM	But ...
UNCLE KEN	The thing is, I'm going to need lots of short walks to make my legs get stronger. There are seven cafes in the High Street, and I've decided to take you all out to tea to a different one every day. It'll be my way of saying thank you.

ICARUS	Ooh, lovely. Thank you very much!
DONUT	Not you, Icarus.
COLIN	Are you sure, Uncle Ken?
MUM	You don't have to do this.
UNCLE KEN	I want to.
CLEO	So do I!
DONUT	And me!
MUM	Well, I'm glad you seem to be back on your feet again.
CLEO	Mum said that all you needed was some Tender Loving Care ...
DONUT	And Tons of Lovely Cakes.
UNCLE KEN	You know what? I think it was the cakes that did it!